Welcome to weights and measures! Here are some words: foot, gallon, ounce, meter, mile, pint, quart, and many more. What do they all mean? Let's start reading and find out.

chicken's foot

elephant's foot

mouse's foot

basketball player's foot

baby's foot

If something is a foot long, how long is it? Is it as long as an elephant's foot? Is it as long as a chicken's foot, a baby's foot, a basketball player's foot? These feet are all different lengths.

ruler

Everyone needs to use the same measurement when describing a distance or a length. Here is a ruler.
It will help us measure things.

inch  1

Here is one inch.
Each piece of candy here is one inch wide.
Two pieces of candy side by side are two inches wide.

Here is a foot. No, not the foot in your shoe!
In this book, a foot is a unit of measure.
Twelve inches equal one foot.

foot

12 inches = 1 foot

12 inches = 1 foot
3 feet = 1 yard
36 inches = 1 yard

yard

If something is a yard long, it does not mean the same thing as the yard behind someone's house. One yard is the same length as three feet. Thirty-six inches is the same as one yard.

mile

1 mile = 1,760 yards
1 mile = 5,280 feet

finish

How long is a mile? It is exactly one thousand seven hundred sixty yards. It is also five thousand two hundred eighty feet. How many HERSHEY'S® Milk Chocolate bars with almonds, placed end to end, would you need to make a mile? You would need more than twelve thousand of them.

metric length measurements

In most countries outside the United States, people do not use inches, feet, yards, or miles. They use a different system of measurement. They use the metric system, which uses different units of measure. If you can count by tens, you can figure out the metric system.

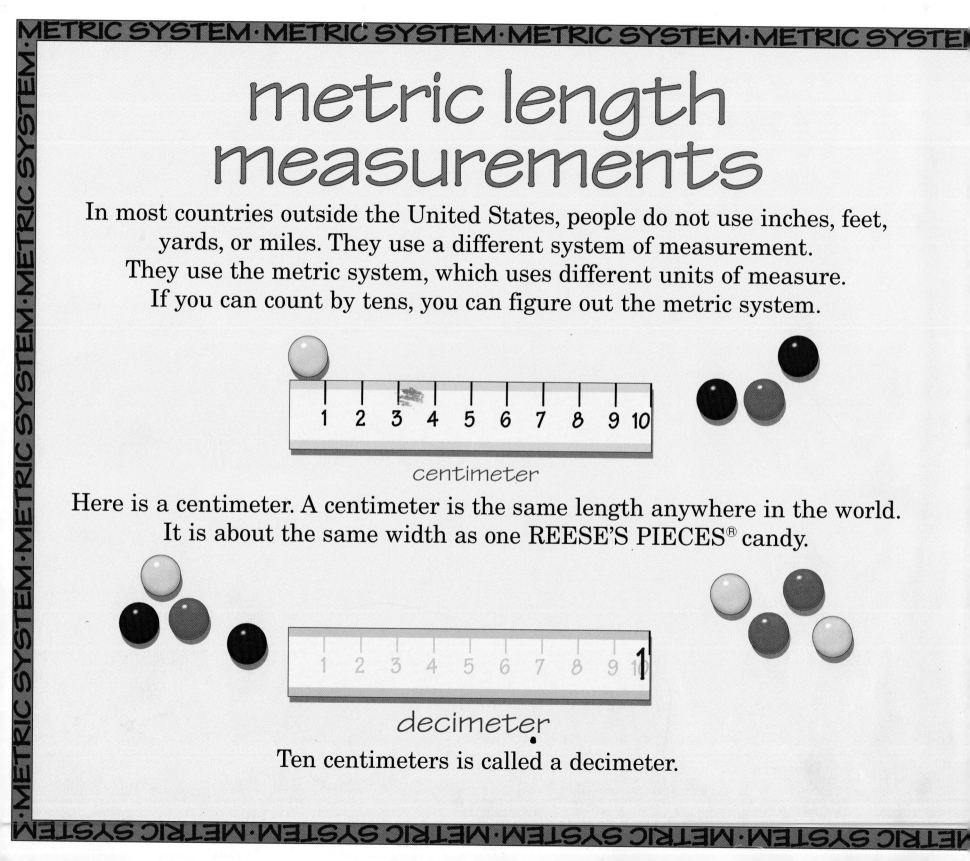

centimeter

Here is a centimeter. A centimeter is the same length anywhere in the world. It is about the same width as one REESE'S PIECES® candy.

decimeter

Ten centimeters is called a decimeter.

How many kilometers is it from your house to school?
How many miles?
Do you walk or take a bus?

meter

One hundred centimeters is a meter.
Ten decimeters is also a meter.
One thousand meters is a kilometer.

That's enough measuring of length or distance! How about weight?
What weighs more: a ton of REESE'S® Peanut Butter Cups,
a ton of feathers, or a ton of lead?

That question was a tricky one!
Do not be fooled by size. They all weigh the same!
A ton is a standard measure. Who would want to eat the feathers anyway?

ounce

Here is one ounce. It is a measure of a specific amount of weight.
There are twelve pieces in a HERSHEY'S Milk Chocolate bar.
Together, eight of the pieces weigh about an ounce.

A pound is sixteen ounces. If someone asks you, "How much do you weigh?"
it is very common to give the answer in pounds.
This bag of TWIZZLERS® Twists weighs one pound.

five pounds

Wow! Here is a HERSHEY'S Milk Chocolate bar that weighs five pounds. The Hershey's Chocolate Factory makes them. The students in your school can share one five-pound bar among themselves.

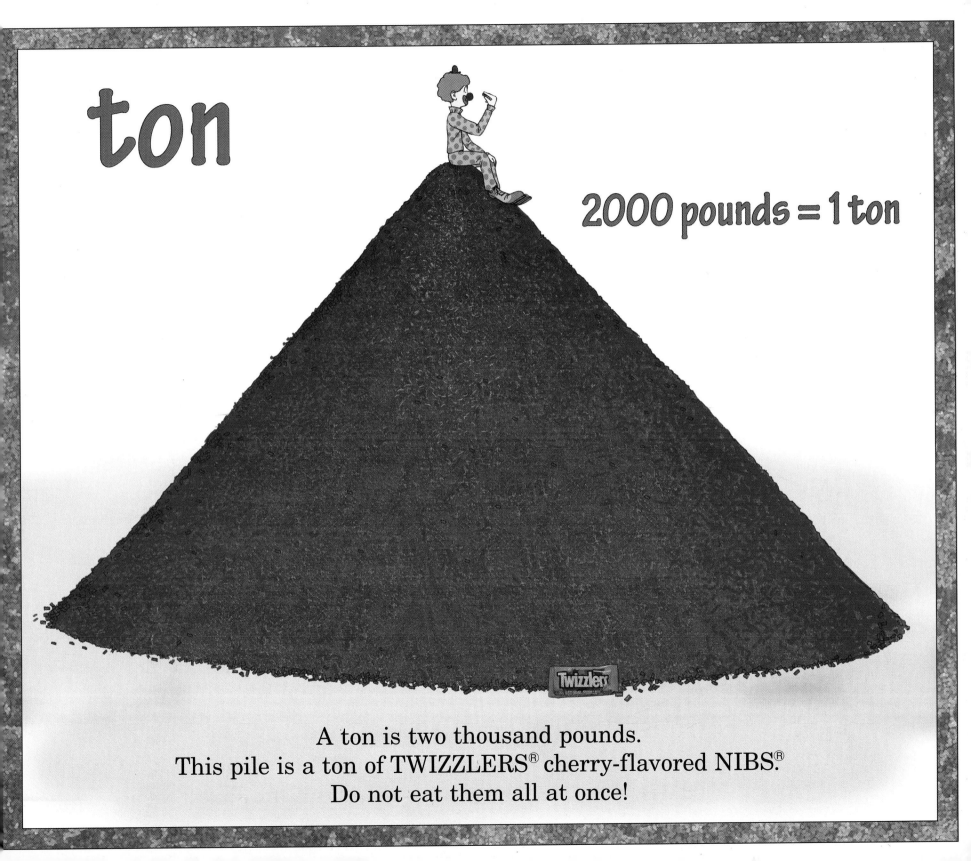

ton

2000 pounds = 1 ton

A ton is two thousand pounds.
This pile is a ton of TWIZZLERS® cherry-flavored NIBS®.
Do not eat them all at once!

metric weight measurement

Remember the metric system?
The metric system also deals with weights.

milligram

Here is a small unit of weight: a milligram.

gram

A thousand milligrams is called a gram. No, not "gram" as in a nickname
for your grandma. A gram is a measure of weight.
The average almond weighs about one gram.

kilogram

1,000 almonds

HERSHEY'S
MILK CHOCOLATE ALMONDS ®

1,000 grams = 1 kilogram

One thousand grams is a kilogram. One thousand kilograms is called a
metric ton. What weighs more, a ton or a metric ton?
The answer is hidden on this page.

What if you ask for some milk?
It is important to say how much you want. If you don't,
you might get a teaspoon, a tablespoon, or a teeny-weeny thimble full.

Or you might get a tanker truck full of milk.
Liquids need to be measured, too. When measuring liquids,
we do not use length or distance. We use volume.

fluid ounce

Here is one fluid ounce of HERSHEY'S Chocolate Syrup.
Let's make chocolate milk!

cup

In this book, a cup does not mean a glass or a cup from your kitchen cabinet.
One cup is eight fluid ounces.
Here is a cup of chocolate milk. Mmmm, delicious!

pint

2 cups = 1 pint
1 pint = 16 ounces

If you drink two cups of chocolate milk, it is the same as drinking a pint. Two cups equal one pint. A pint is also equal to sixteen ounces.

quart

2 pints = 1 quart
4 cups = 1 quart
1 quart = 32 ounces

Waiter, waiter, I would like to order one quart of chocolate milk, please.
Two pints equal one quart. Four cups equal one quart.

gallon

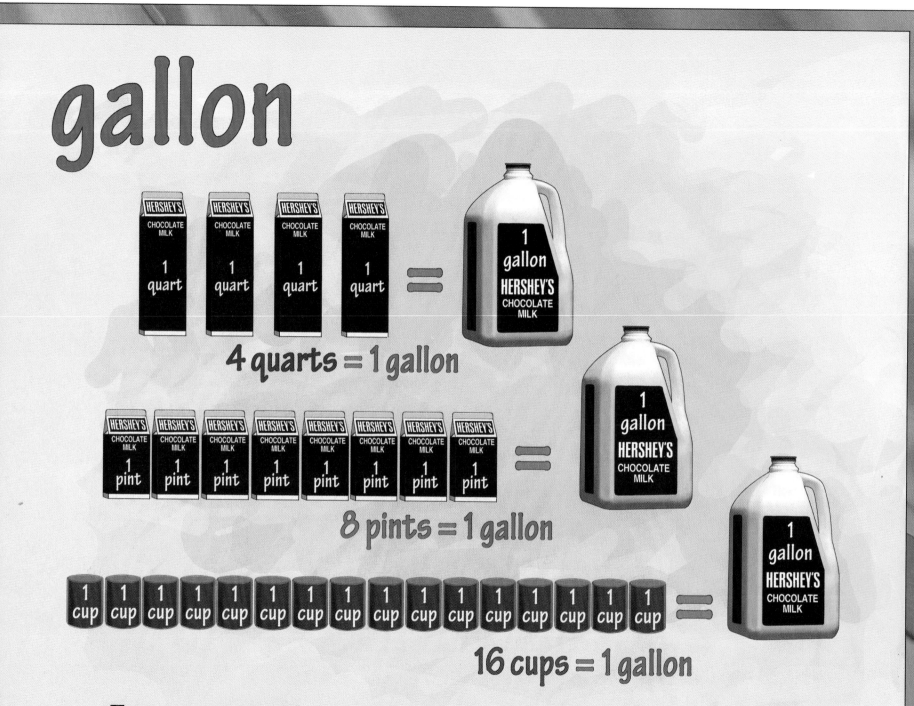

4 quarts = 1 gallon

8 pints = 1 gallon

16 cups = 1 gallon

Four quarts equal one gallon. One quart is a quarter of a gallon. That's where the word "quart" comes from. How many pints are in a gallon? How many cups?

billions of gallons

HERSHEY'S

How many gallons of water are in the ocean? Billions and billions and billions of gallons. What if the ocean were made of chocolate milk? The whales probably wouldn't like it.

metric liquid measurement

There is a metric system for liquids, too. The system is based on the liter as the unit of measure.

milliliter  Here is one milliliter.

 Ten milliliters equal a centiliter.

One hundred centiliters equal a liter.

1 liter

Many different types of drinks are sold in one-liter bottles.

kiloliter

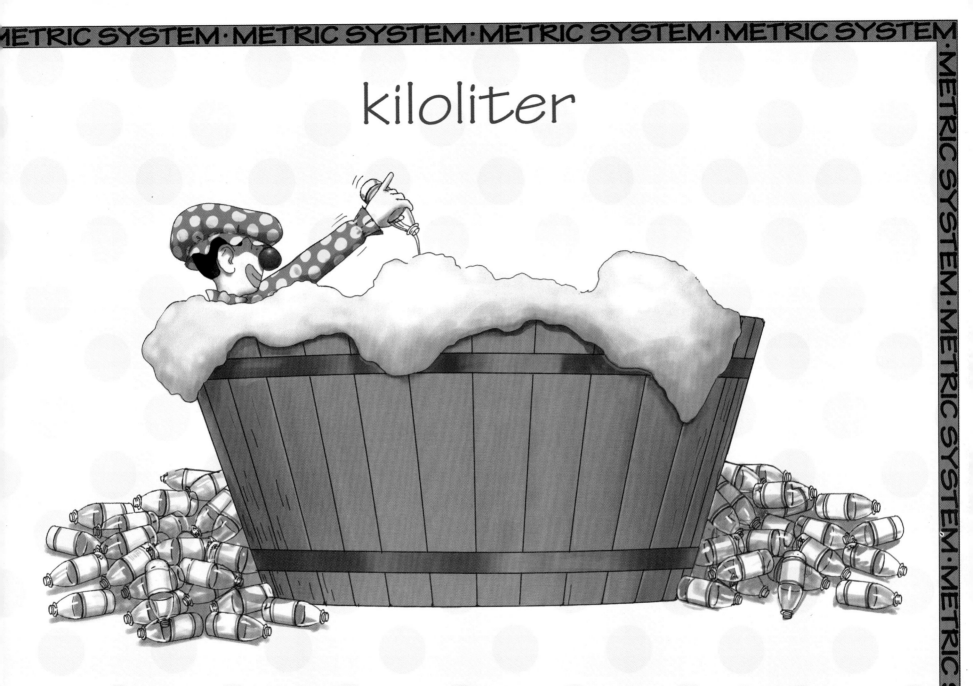

One thousand liters is called a kiloliter.
How many liters would it take to fill this tub?

time

second

minute hour

60 seconds = 1 minute
60 minutes = 1 hour
24 hours = 1 day

There is another thing we measure.
It is called time! How long did it take to read this book?
Did it take a second, a minute, or an hour?

week **year**

day

7 days = 1 week
52 weeks = 1 year
12 months = 1 year

There are twenty-four hours in one day. There are seven days in one week.
There are fifty-two weeks in one year. There are also twelve months in one year.
Did it take you one year to read this book?
There is no such thing as *metric time*.

Here is something we cannot measure.
We cannot measure how much you love reading.
We hope you always love to read!